I0469868

This book belongs to:

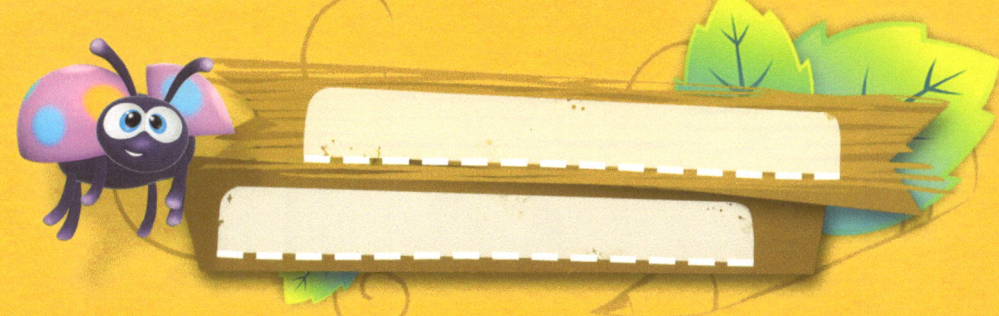

How to use this book?

This book is here for you to learn, improve your drawing and coloring skills and, of course, have fun!

Meet our amazing colorbug characters and they will tell you some cool facts about their species. Have fun drawing them, coloring them and bringing them to life using the colorbug app which you can download on Google Play, App Store or directly from our website getcolorbug.com

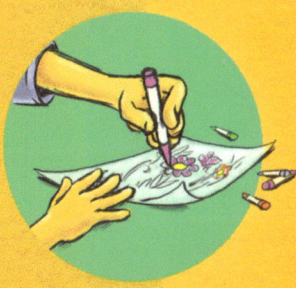

Wherever you see this sign:

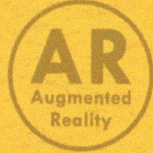

AR
Augmented Reality

point your device at the image and experience the magic of Augmented Reality!

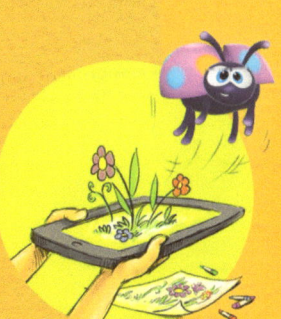

Designed and developed by
pixelbug

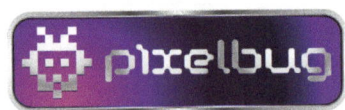

Contact:
info@pixelbug.com
pixelbug.com

P.O. Box 341399
Dubai, United Arab Emirates

©2015 pixelbug - all rights reserved

Meet Bugsy

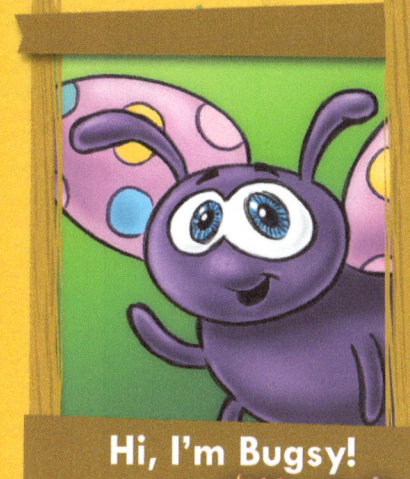

Hi, I'm Bugsy!

Bugsy is a ladybug. She loves flowers and nature. She is a very friendly creature, and has a lot of friends in the animal kingdom. She's really smart because she reads many books. To some of her friends, she seems like she knows everything about everything.

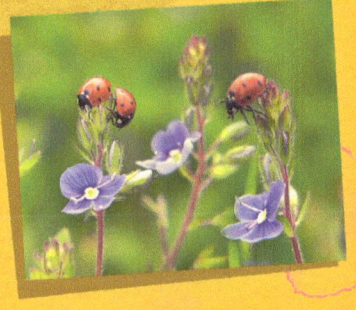

Ladybugs

Did you know that ladybugs aren't really bugs at all? They are beetles! Scientists usually prefer to call them lady beetles. They are commonly yellow, orange, or scarlet with small black spots on their wing covers and black legs, heads and antennae.

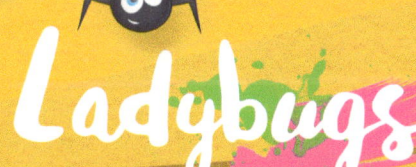

Ladybugs cannot see colors at all. They can only see the difference between dark and light, as if everything was a black and white photo. When the ladybugs fly, they beat their wings 5100 times in a minute. That is almost 85 beats in a second!

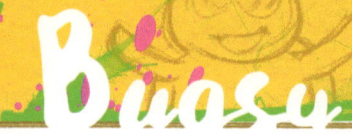

Draw your own Bugsy following these steps!

 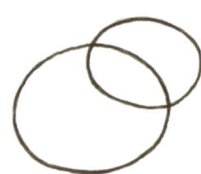

 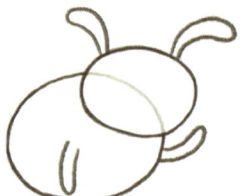 

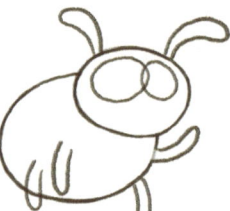

 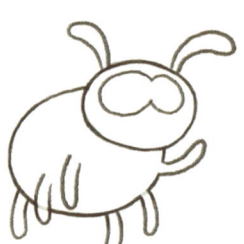

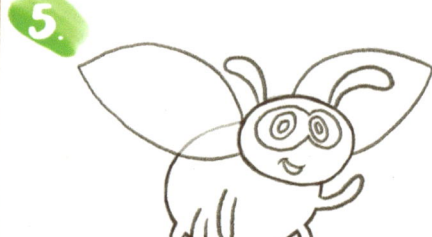

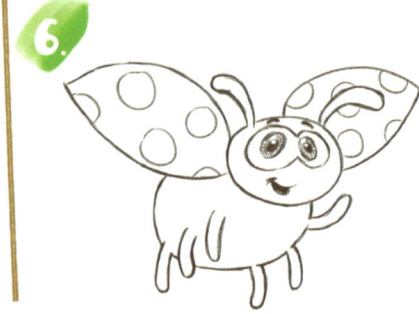

Spot 5 differences!

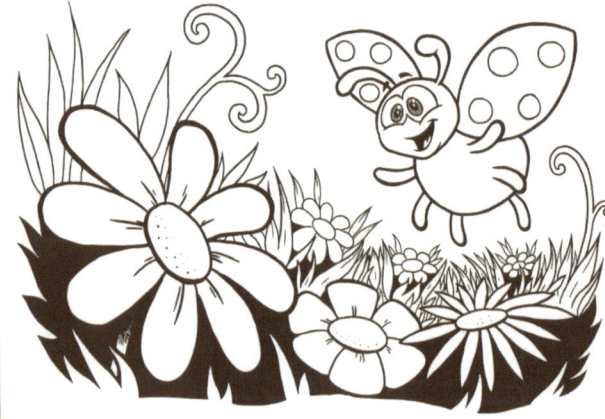

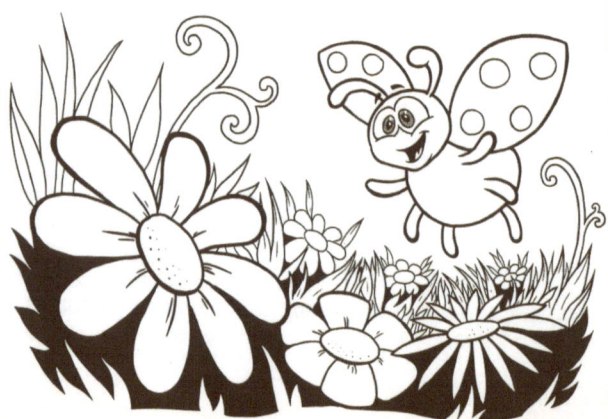

Fill the vase with flowers!

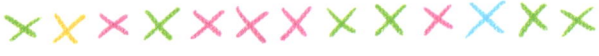

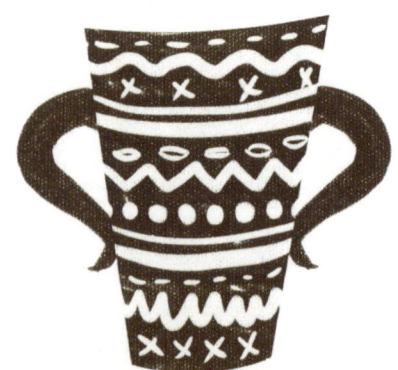

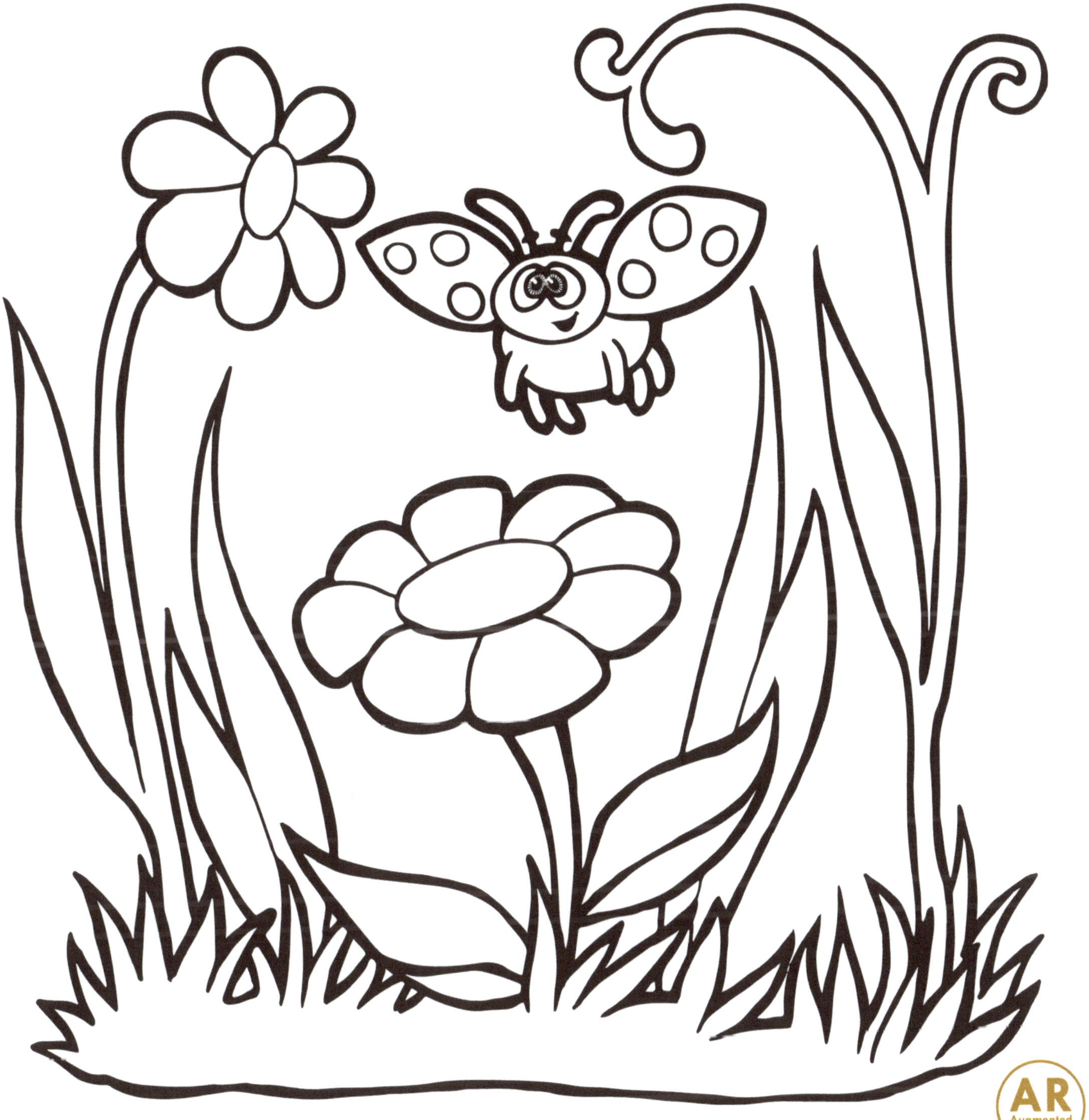

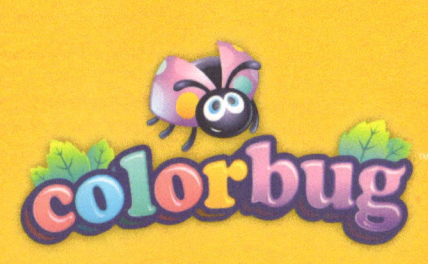

an augmented reality edutainment app that magically brings kids' storytelling and coloring books, to life!

getcolorbug.com

AR
Augmented
Reality

A space for your sketches, drawings and doodles

Meet Ricky

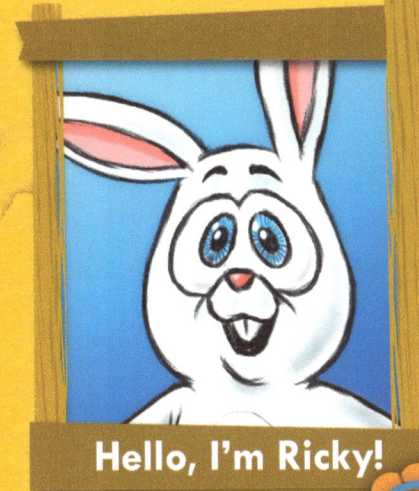

Hello, I'm Ricky!

1st

Ricky is not just any kind of rabbit, he's also an Easter rabbit. During Easter, he travels around the world and gives Easter eggs to everyone and then spends the rest of the year playing sports. It's no wonder that he is the two legged running champion of the animal kingdom. He also enjoys listening to music, especially hip hop, which is his favorite genre. He also likes taking selfies in front of world famous landmarks, especially with the Statue of Liberty in New York, his hometown.

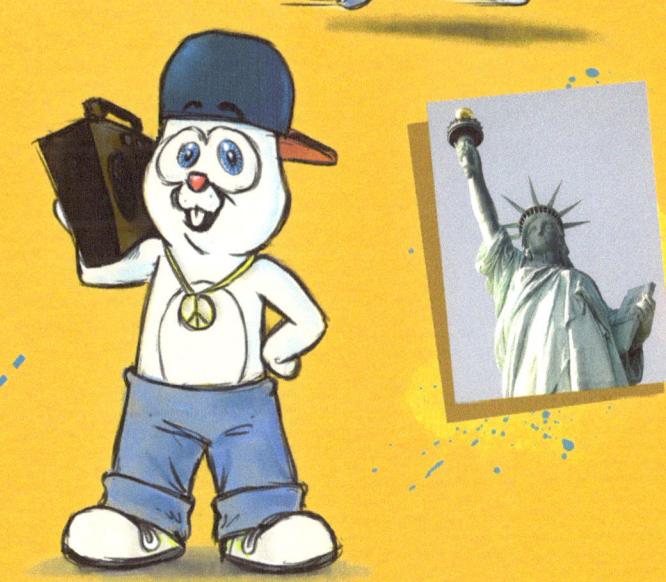

Rabbits

Rabbits are small mammals that live in groups. Their habitats include meadows, woods, forests, grasslands, deserts and wetlands. Rabbits have nearly 360° panoramic vision, allowing them to detect predators from all directions.

Rabbits have two sets of incisor teeth, one behind the other. This way they can be distinguished from rodents, with which they are often confused. Did you know that rabbits can be trained? Much like a dog, a pet rabbit can be taught to come to his/her name, sit in your lap, and do simple tricks!

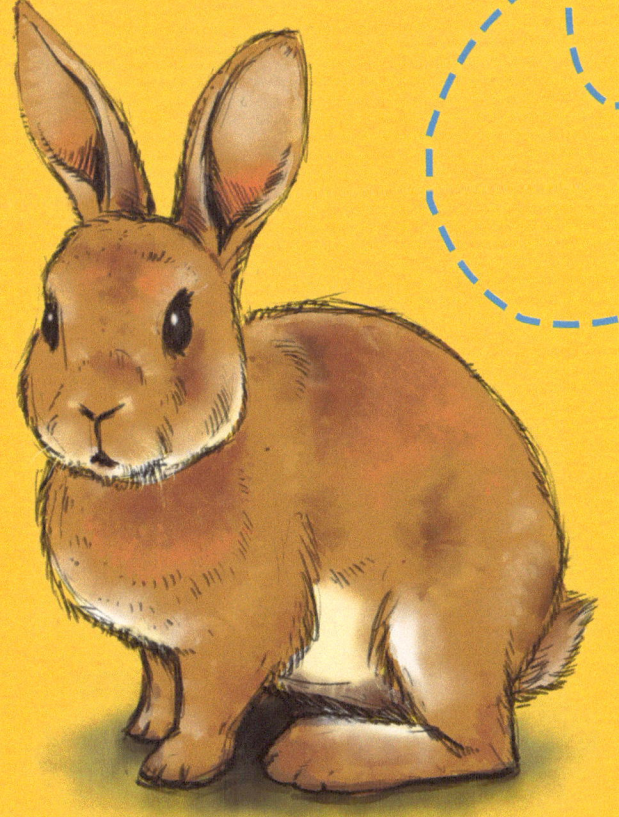

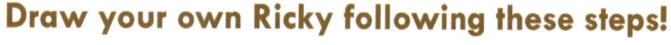

Fun with Ricky

Draw your own Ricky following these steps!

 1.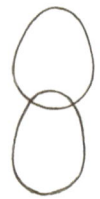

 2.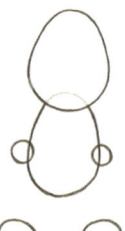

 3.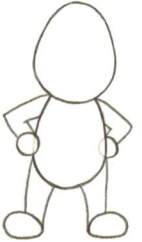

 4.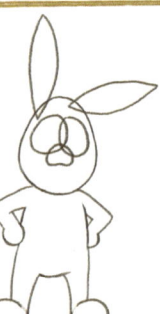

5.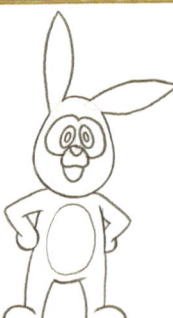

 6.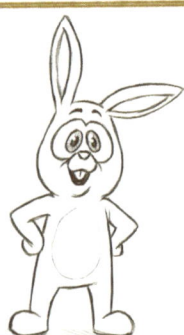

Connect the dots!

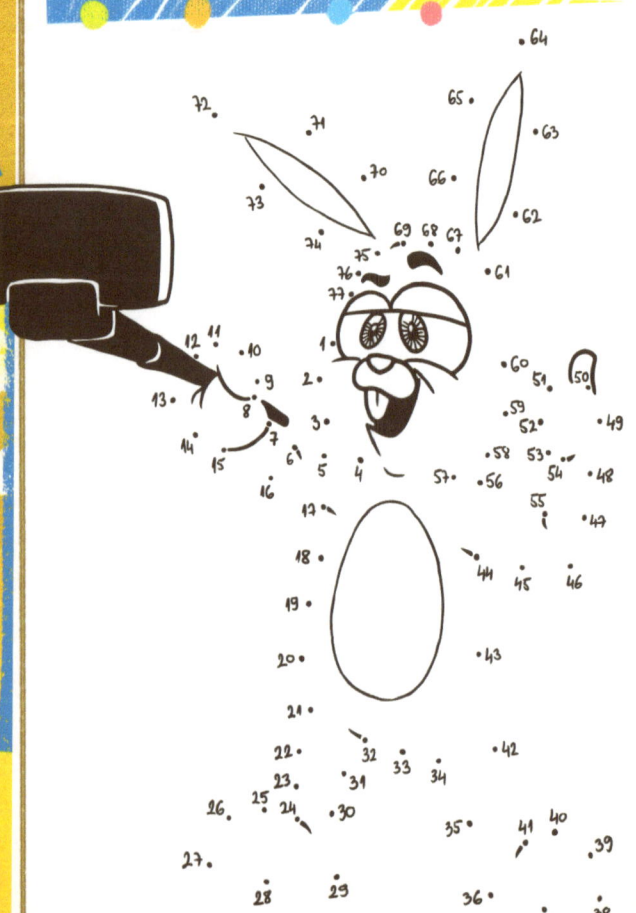

Connect the pictures with the correct names!

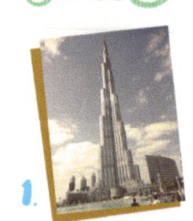
1.

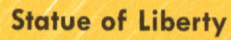
Statue of Liberty

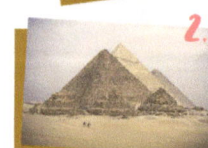
2.

Eiffel Tower

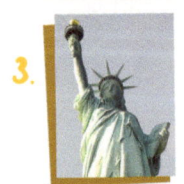
3.

Sydney Opera

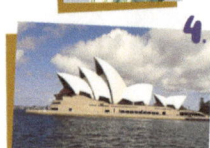
4.

Burj Khalifa

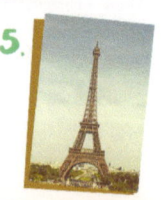
5.

Pyramids of Giza

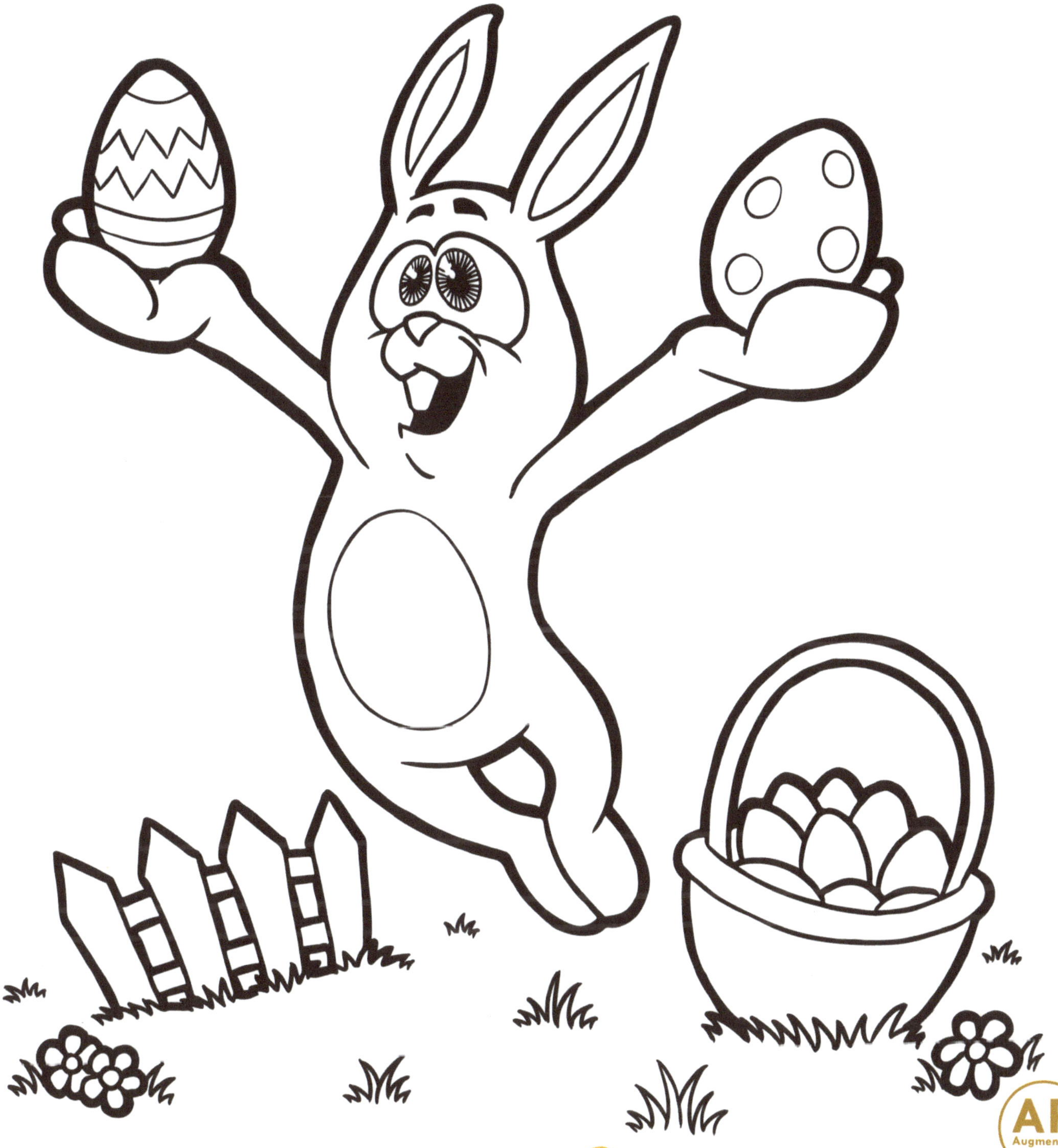

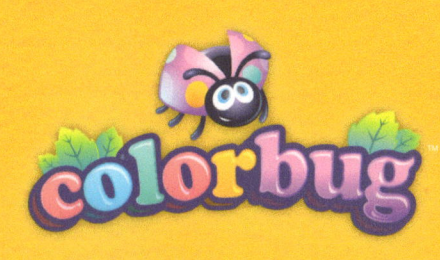

an augmented reality
edutainment app that magically
brings kids' storytelling
and coloring books,
to life!

getcolorbug.com

AR
Augmented
Reality

A space for your sketches, drawings and doodles

Meet Mushrif

Mushrif is a...well, a plant. But he is a very special plant. He's a friendly veggie and he lives in Abu Dhabi's Mushrif Central Park. He is the park's community ambassador; he is fun-loving, friendly and helpful. Mushrif appreciates nature and loves sharing his passion with different members of the community. He also cares about the environment, promotes respecting the park and leading an active and healthy lifestyle.

Hi, I'm Mushrif!

Mushrif Central Park

Mushrif Central Park is a park for all the people of Abu Dhabi. Bringing together communities in a safe and secure environment. Creating opportunities to explore, experience, enrich and educate through a vibrant range of facilities. Mushrif Central Park was first opened to visitors in 1982. It is one of the oldest and largest urban parks in Abu Dhabi. Since its opening, the park has been a community hub for generations of Abu Dhabi locals and residents.

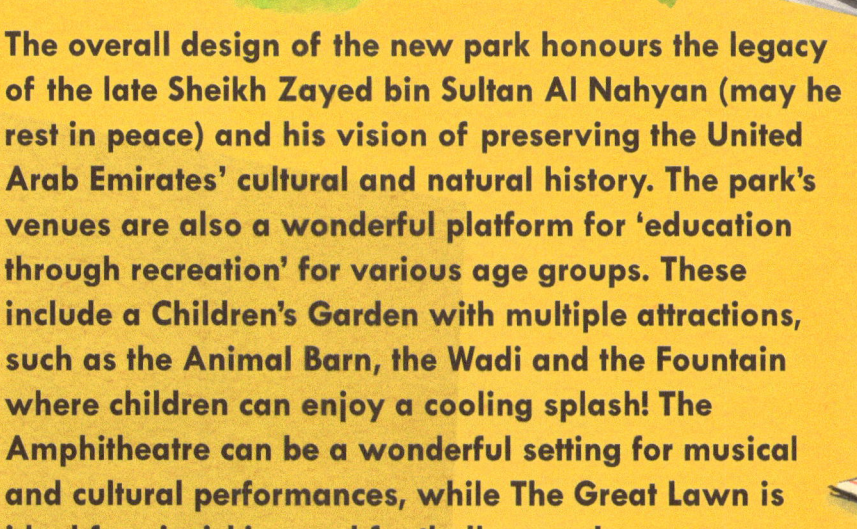

The overall design of the new park honours the legacy of the late Sheikh Zayed bin Sultan Al Nahyan (may he rest in peace) and his vision of preserving the United Arab Emirates' cultural and natural history. The park's venues are also a wonderful platform for 'education through recreation' for various age groups. These include a Children's Garden with multiple attractions, such as the Animal Barn, the Wadi and the Fountain where children can enjoy a cooling splash! The Amphitheatre can be a wonderful setting for musical and cultural performances, while The Great Lawn is ideal for picnicking and football games!

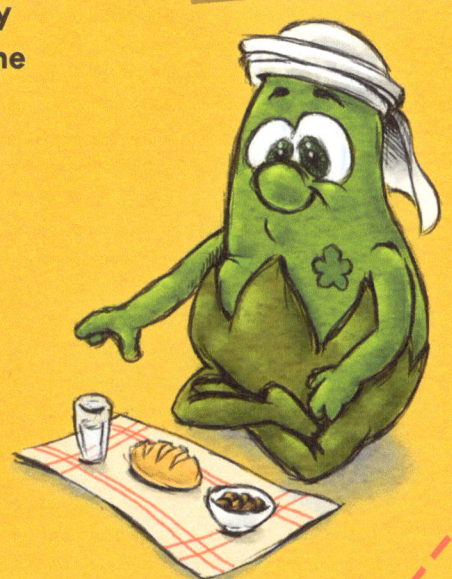

Draw your own Mushrif following these steps!

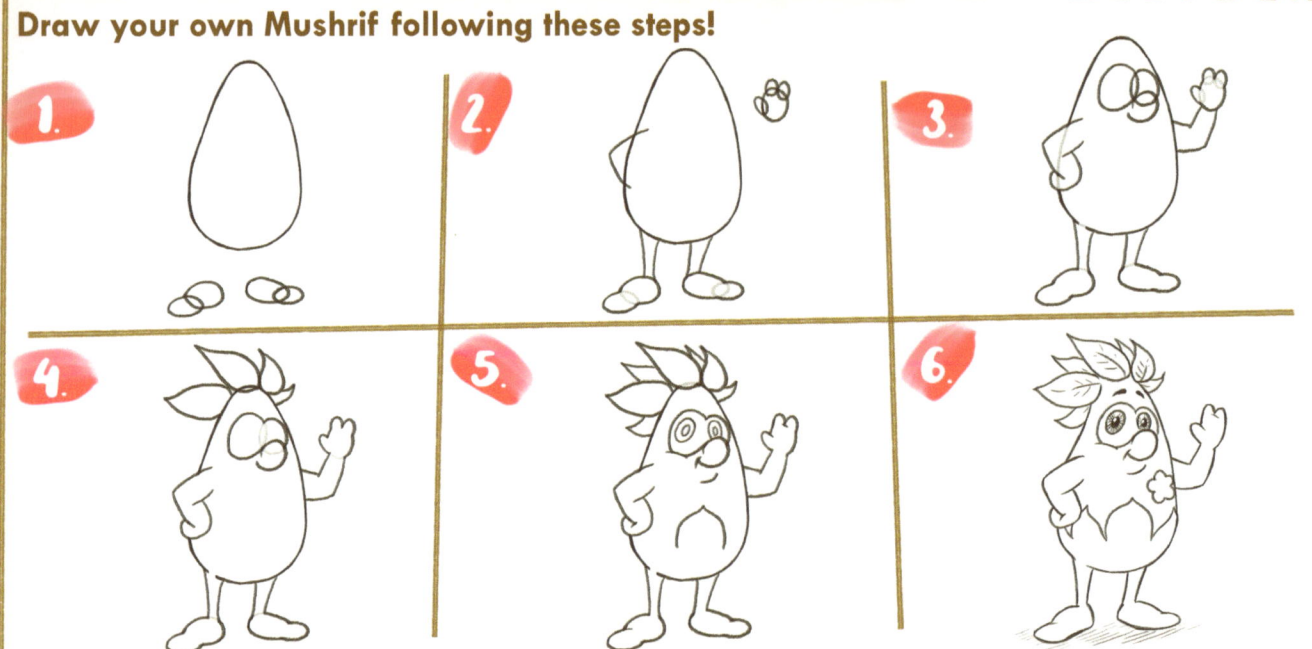

Every row, column and grid must contain all four of these images:

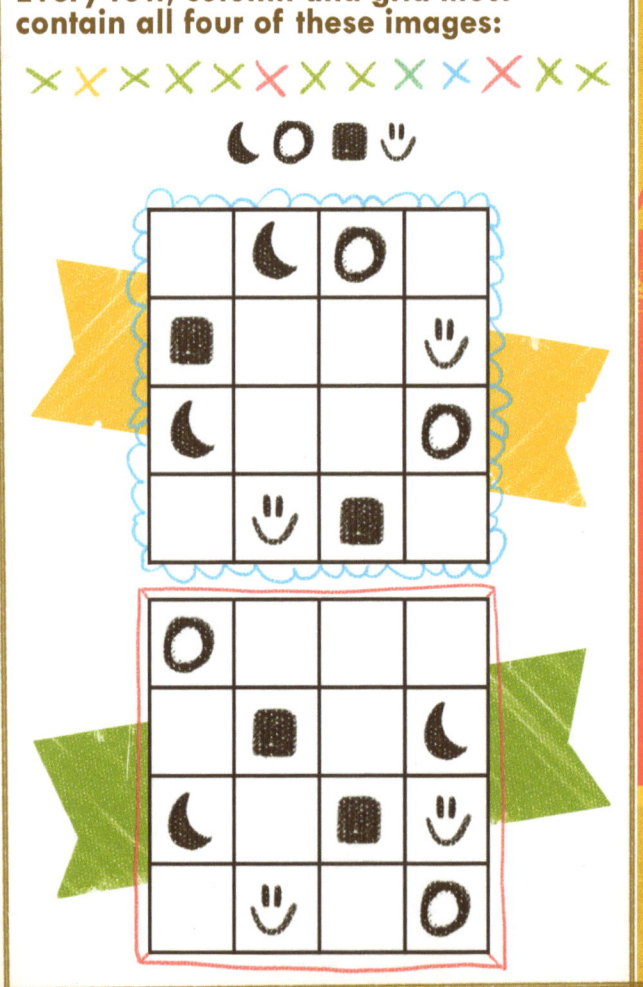

Decode the message!

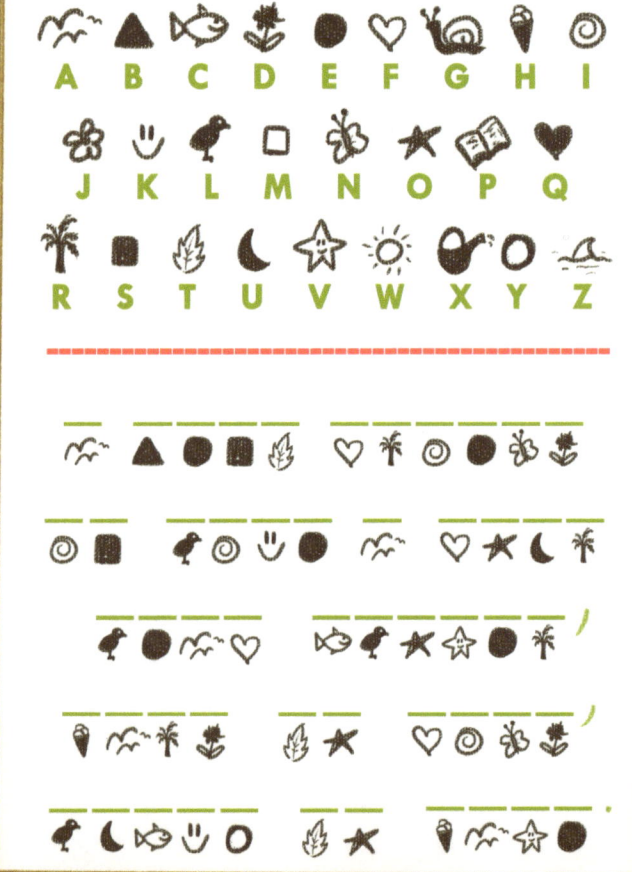

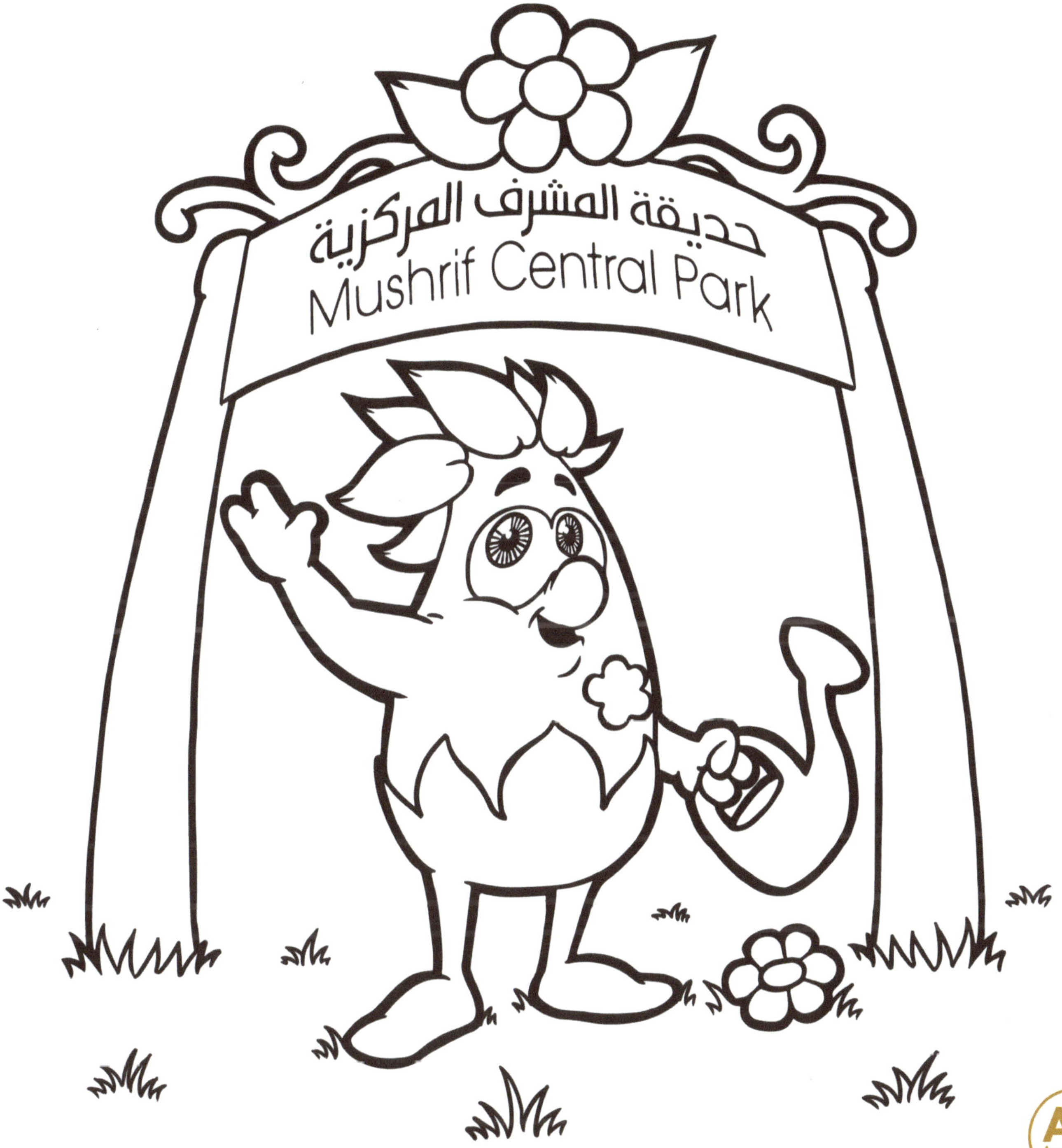

حديقة المشرف المركزية
Mushrif Central Park

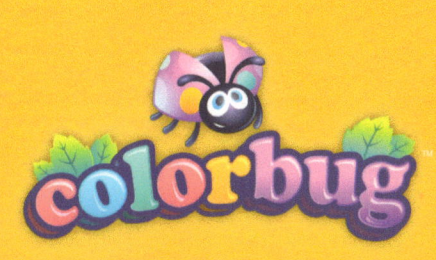

an augmented reality edutainment app that magically brings kids' storytelling and coloring books, to life!

AR Augmented Reality

getcolorbug.com

A space for your sketches, drawings and doodles

Meet Patrick

Patrick comes from Paris and is very artistic. He loves to paint and listen to classical music on the radio. He is elegant and proudly trots under the Eiffel Tower. Besides art he also likes sports, especially football. He considers football to be not just a sport, but a form of art. He's a wannabe football player, and his role model is the great French player Michel Platini.

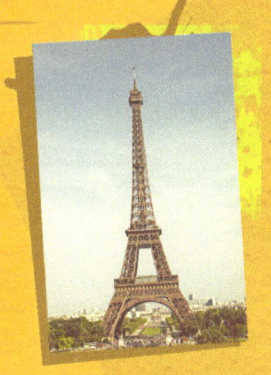

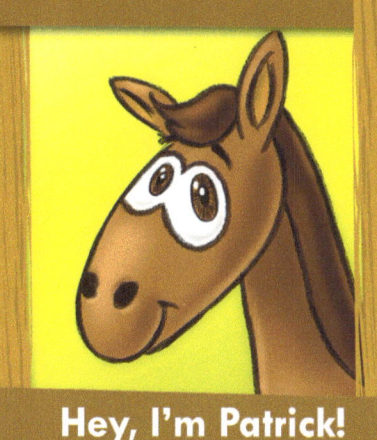

Hey, I'm Patrick!

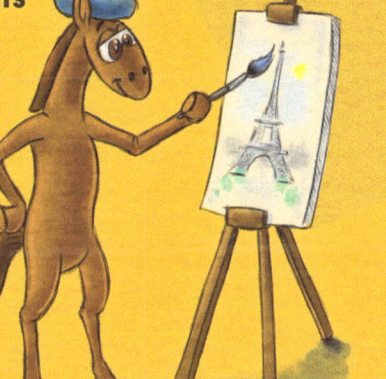

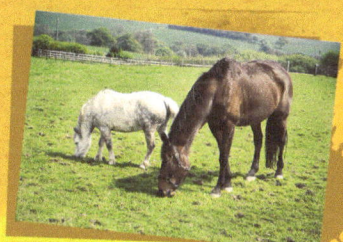

Horses

Horses are mammals with a life expectancy of 25 to 30 years. Horses have around 250 bones in their skeleton and are very strong animals. Because horses have eyes on the side of their head they can see nearly 360 degrees at one time. They can sleep both lying down and standing up. Female horses, called mares, carry their young for approximately 11 months, and a young horse, called a foal, can stand and run shortly following birth. Horses have 16 muscles in each ear, allowing them to rotate their ears 180 degrees. Did you know that horses have bigger eyes than any other mammal that lives on land? They have excellent day and night vision and a sense of smell better than that of humans.

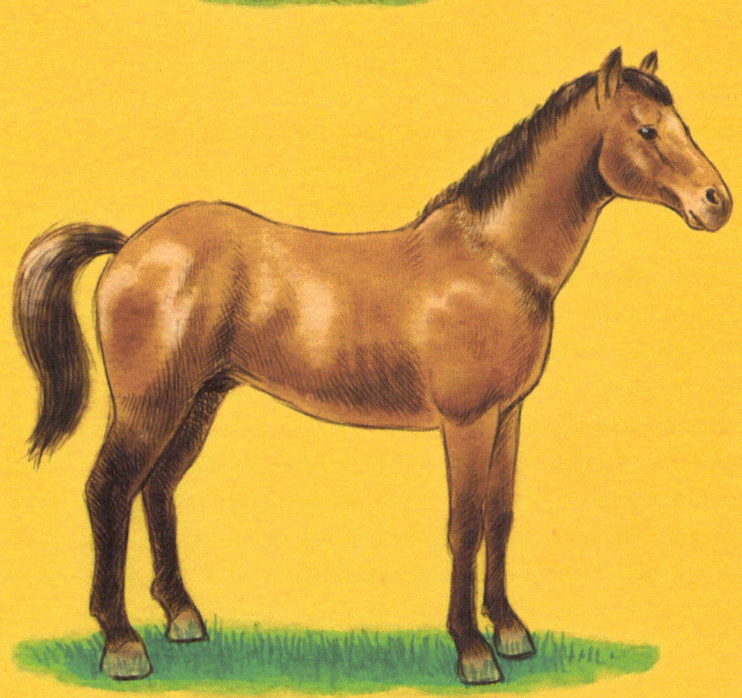

Fun with Patrick

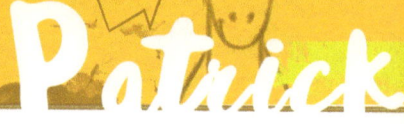

Draw your own Patrick following these steps!

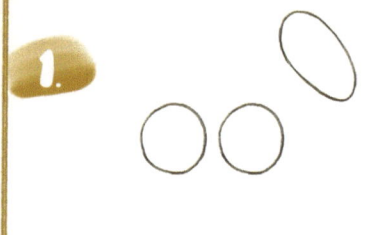
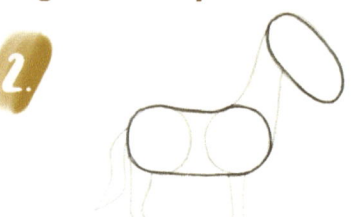
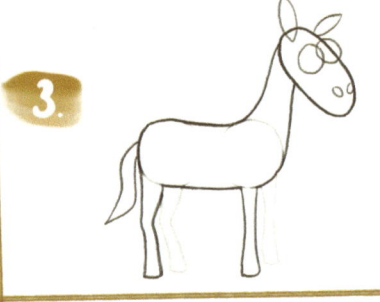
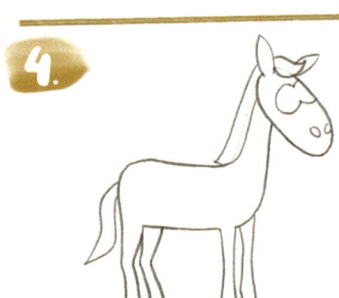
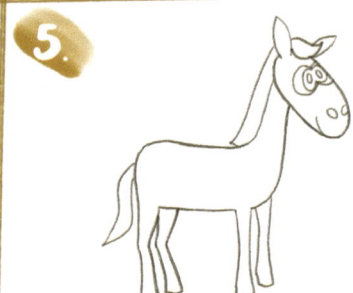
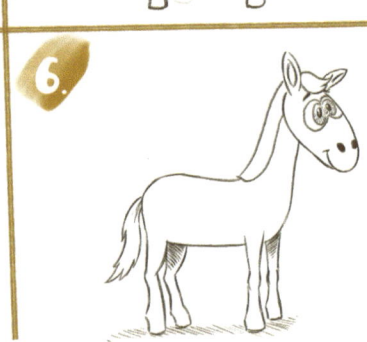

Help Patrick find his ball!

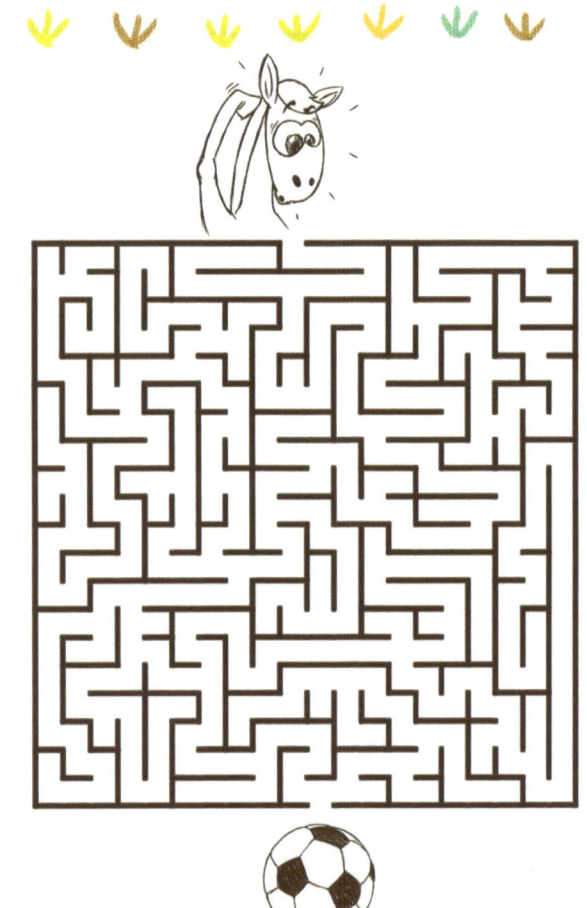

Take some watercolors, mix them and paint the circles with the colors that you get!

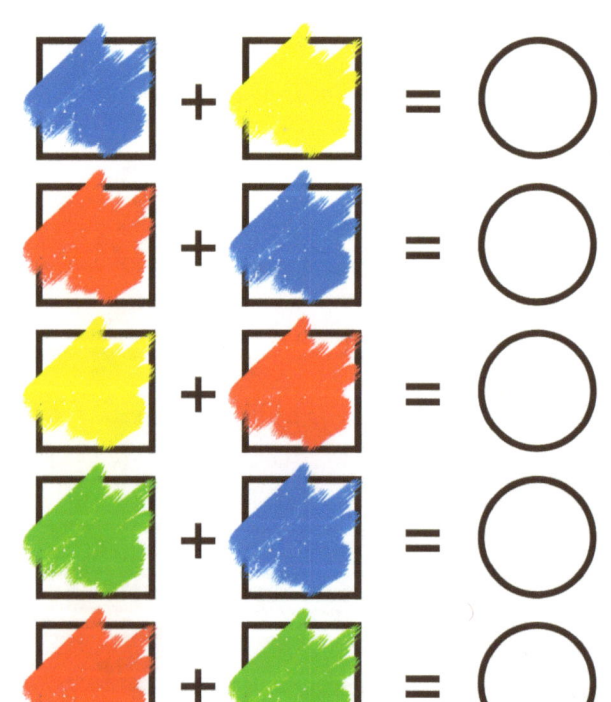

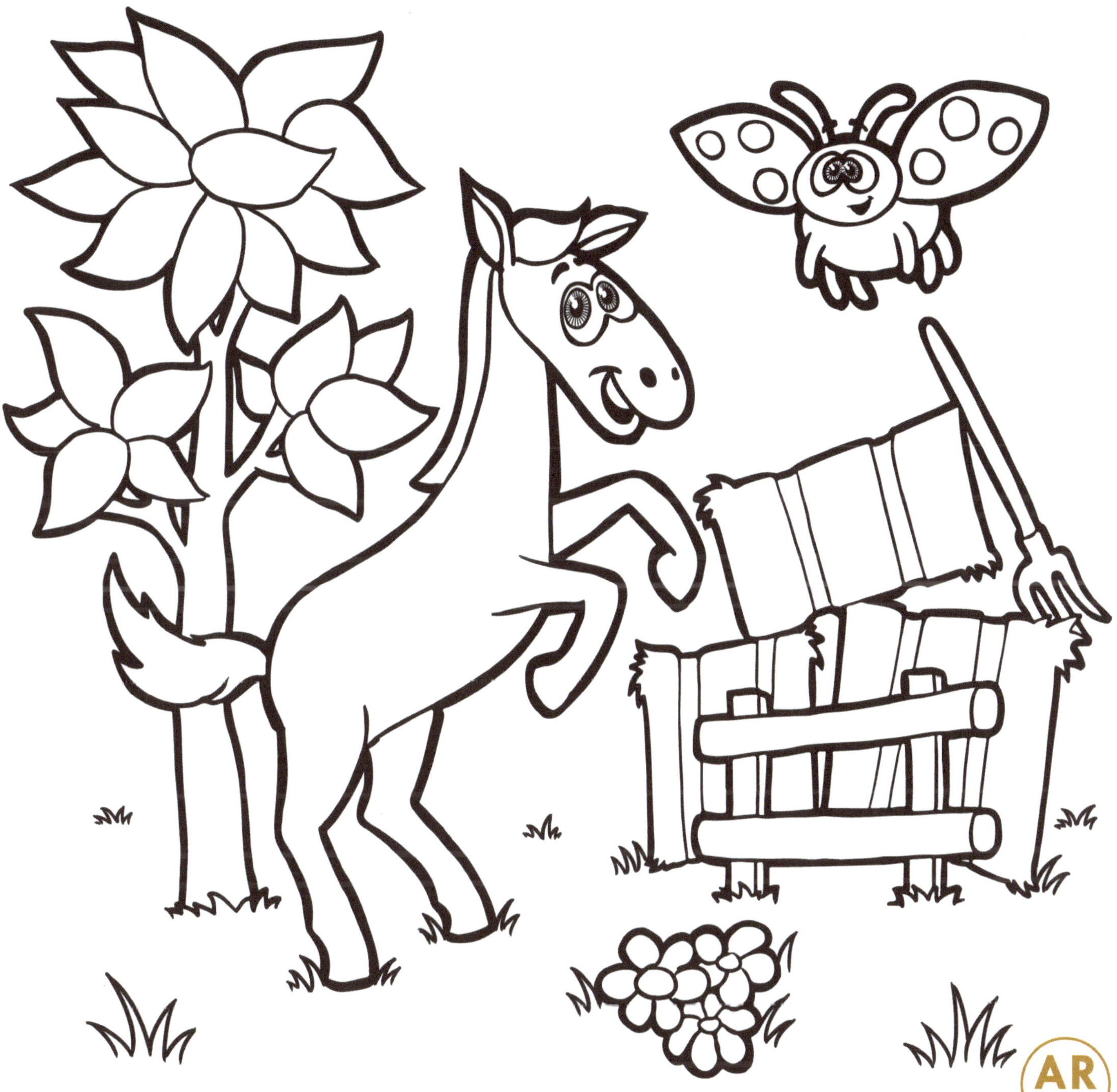

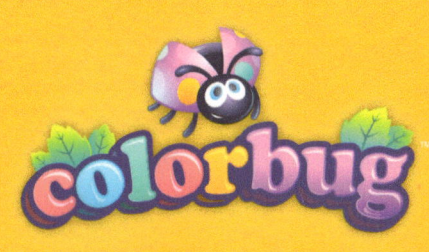

an augmented reality edutainment app that magically brings kids' storytelling and coloring books, to life!

AR
Augmented
Reality

getcolorbug.com

A space for your sketches, drawings and doodles

Meet Pablo

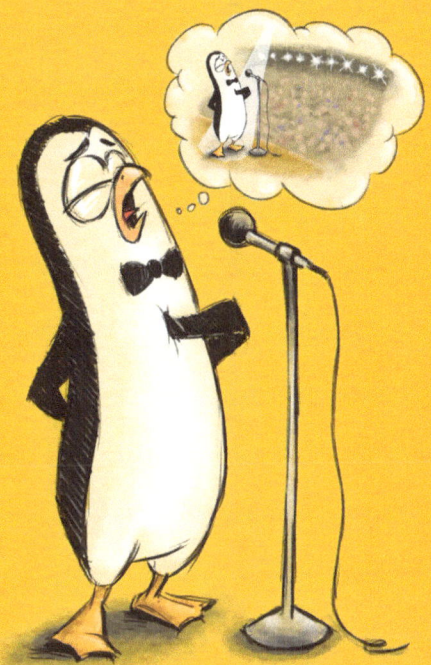

Pablo is an odd kind of penguin; he is from the Antarctica yet he prefers warmer climates. He enjoys the sun, scuba diving, fishing and traveling. One of his favorite destinations is Australia. He also loves to sing opera, and says that one day he'll be singing like the great Pavarotti. He dreams of singing in front of the full Sydney Opera House someday.

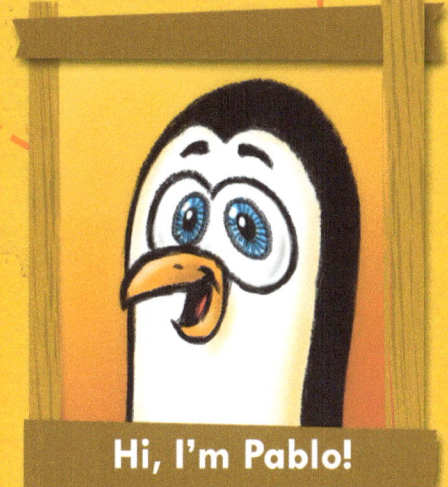

Hi, I'm Pablo!

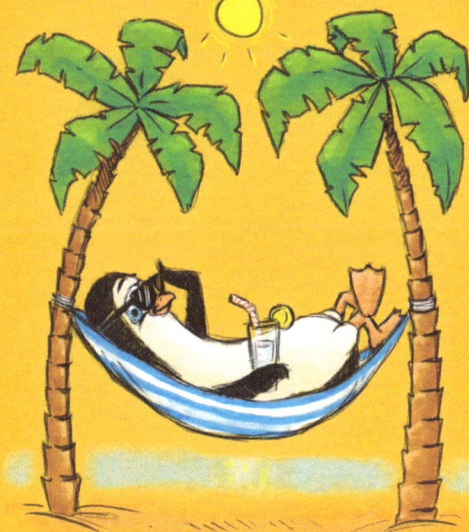

Penguins

Penguins are a group of aquatic birds living almost exclusively in the Southern Hemisphere, especially in Antarctica. They cannot fly with their wings, instead, they have adapted flippers to help them swim in the water.

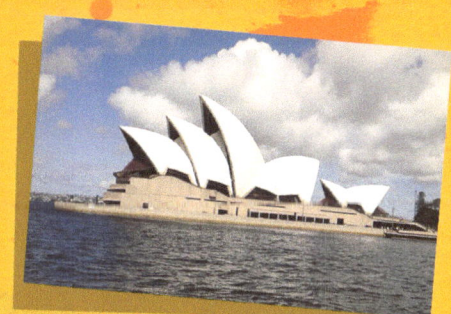

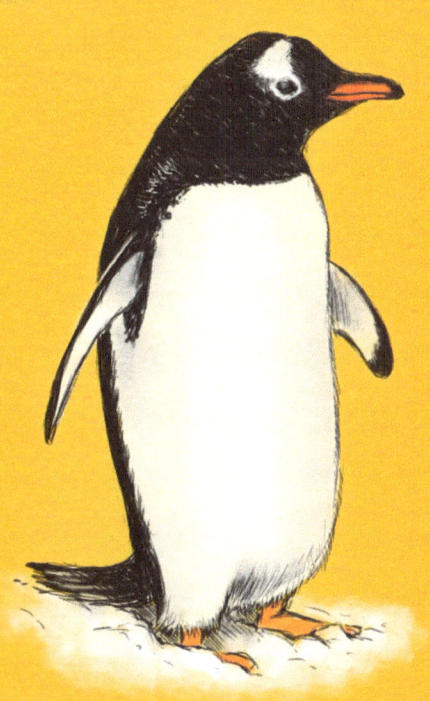

A penguin swimming looks very similar to a bird's flight in the air. On land, penguins use their tails and wings to maintain balance for their upright stance. The emperor penguin is the tallest of all penguin species, reaching as tall as 120 cm in height. Did you know that they can stay underwater for around 20 minutes at a time? Penguins' eyes actually work better underwater than they do in the air! They can drink seawater and they eat a range of fish and other sea life.

Fun with Pablo

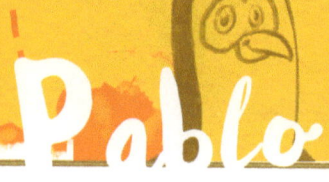

Draw your own Pablo following these steps!

1.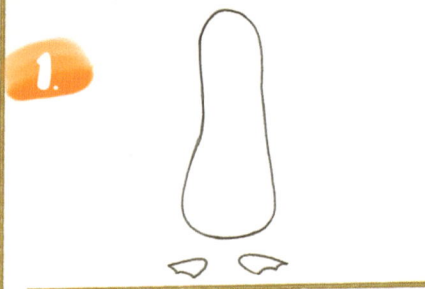
2.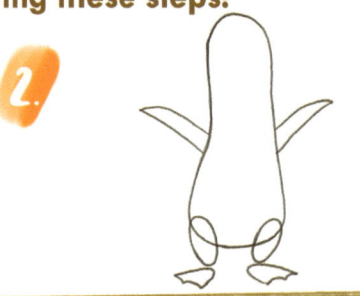
3.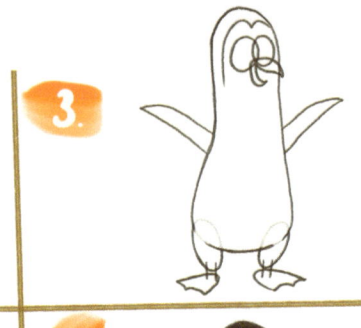
4.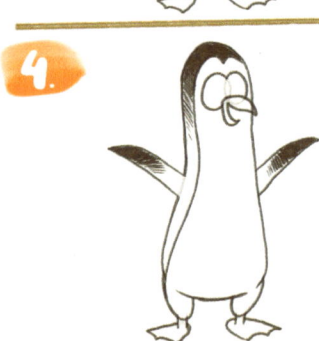
5.
6.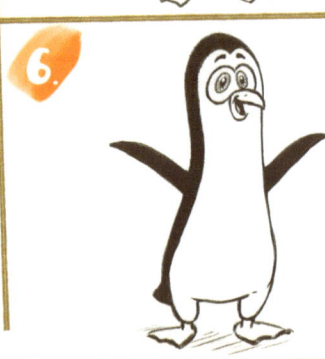

Which two fish are the same?

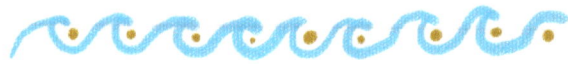

1.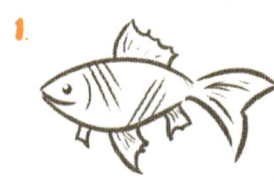
2.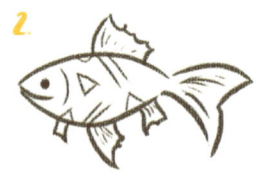
3.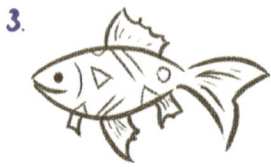
4.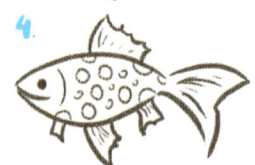
5.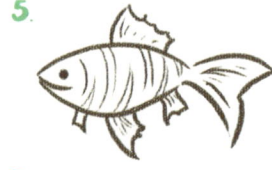
6.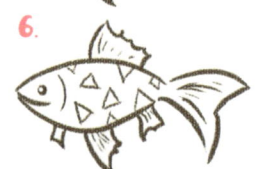
7.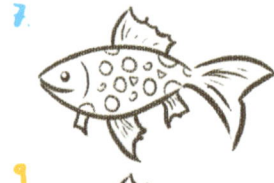
8.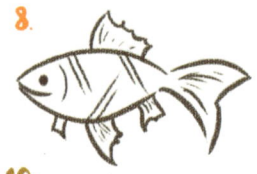
9.
10.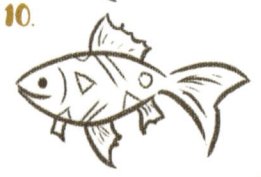

Write down the names of the instruments!

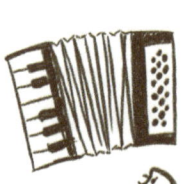

_____

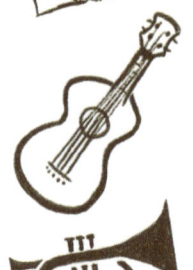

_____

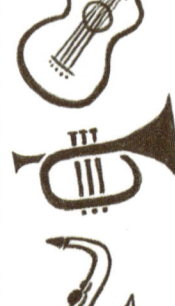

_____

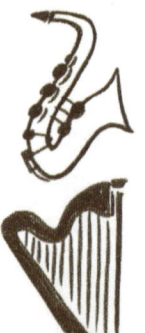

_____

_____

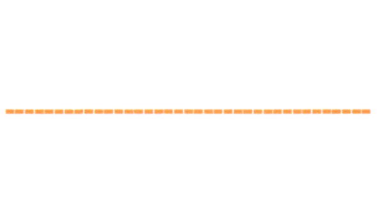

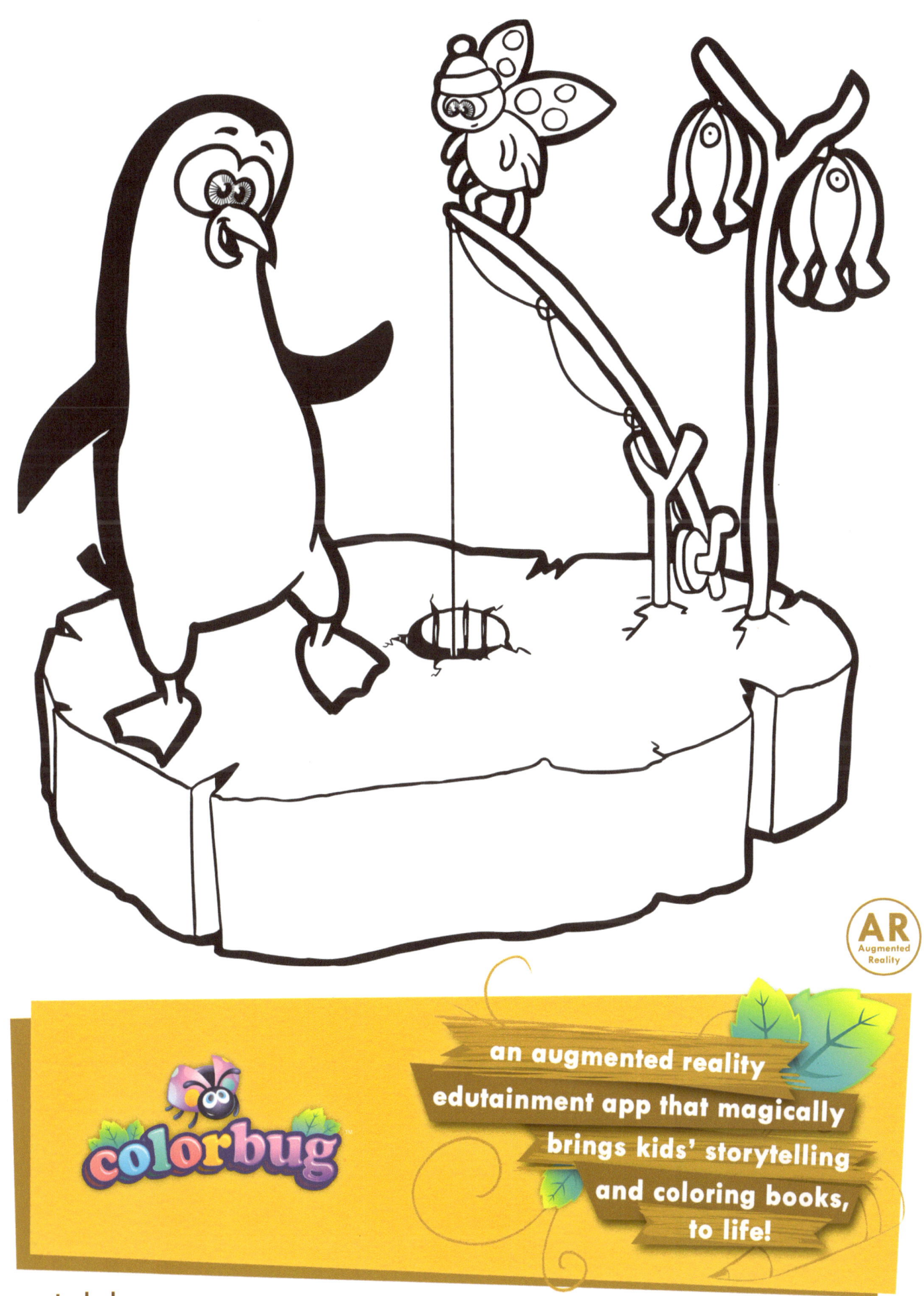

colorbug

an augmented reality edutainment app that magically brings kids' storytelling and coloring books, to life!

getcolorbug.com

A space for your sketches, drawings and doodles

Meet Clemence

To be exact, Clemence is an Arabian camel. She is very wise and patient. She likes history, archeology and ancient structures. One of her favorite archeological sites is Giza and its pyramids. She loves the desert and loves to lay under the sun. However, she doesn't like sandstorms or desert winds, which make her all sneezy because of her sensitive nose.

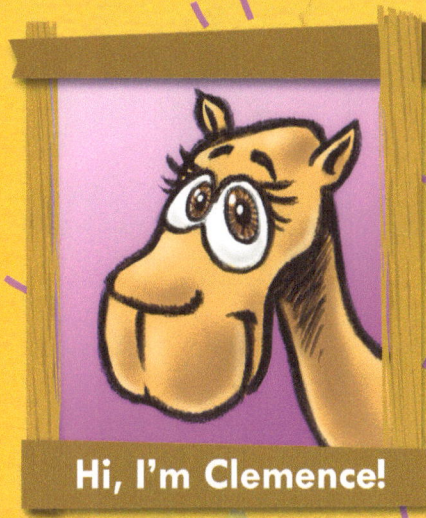

Hi, I'm Clemence!

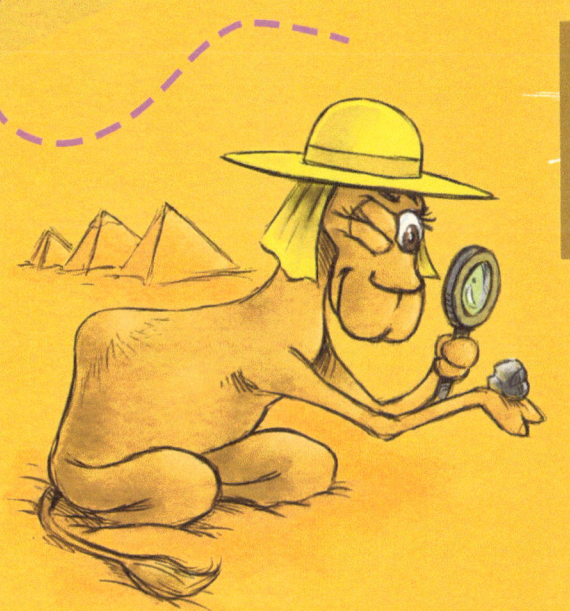

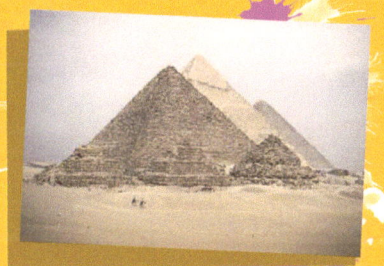

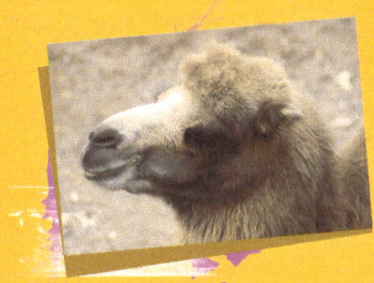

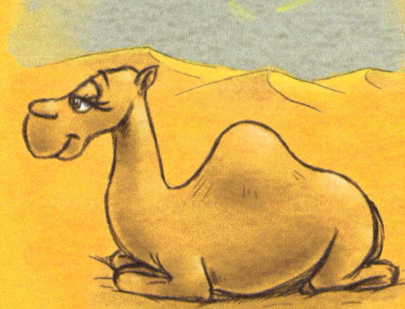

Camels

The average life expectancy of a camel is 40 to 50 years. The Arabian camel has only one hump while Asian camels have two. Did you know that camels do not store water in their humps? The humps are actually reservoirs for fatty tissue which helps camels to survive in such extremely hot regions. Camels have played an important role in Arabian culture and there are over 160 words for 'camel' in the Arabic language. In Arab cultures the camel symbolises patience, tolerance and endurance. The earliest known camel lived in North America 40 to 50 million years ago.

Fun with Clemence

Clemence

Draw your own Clemence following these steps!

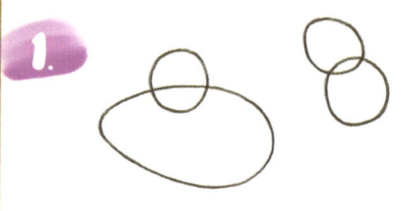
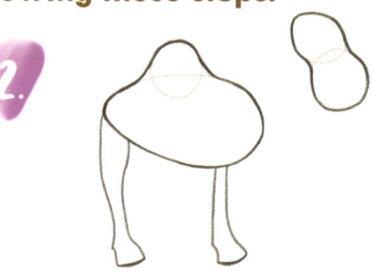
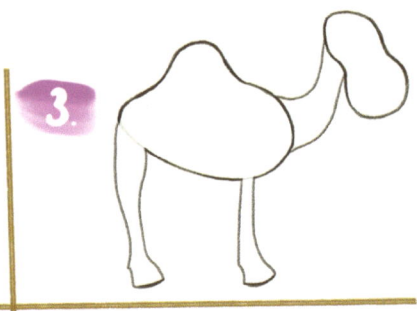
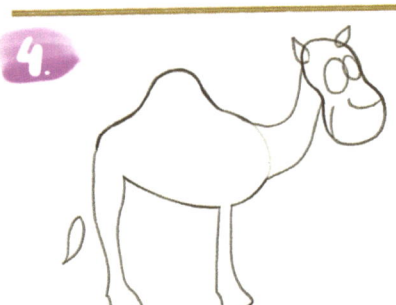
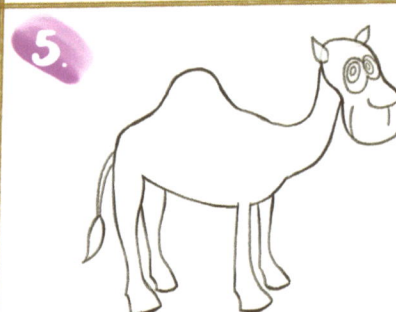
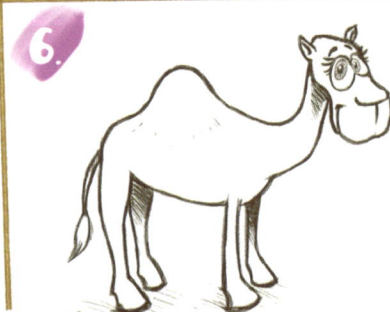

Find the words!

CAMEL   PYRAMIDS

ARCHEOLOGY   SANDSTORM   DESERT

TOLERANCE   HISTORY

```
D P F C A M E L X G
A V I C V G O O G L
N A M H Q U L C X E
D Q R C F R D U B T
S Z I C R I G F A H
A C N E N C T M R X
N T O L E R T A C H
D E S E R T Y P H E
S D M T S Y Y A E Q
T Q V G T E R W O H
O O M T P B A Z L I
R I P Y P Y M Q O S
M J M V A X I I G T
X E Y L R W D W Y O
E J W P Z H S M D Y
```

Color in fields using the colors of the dots.

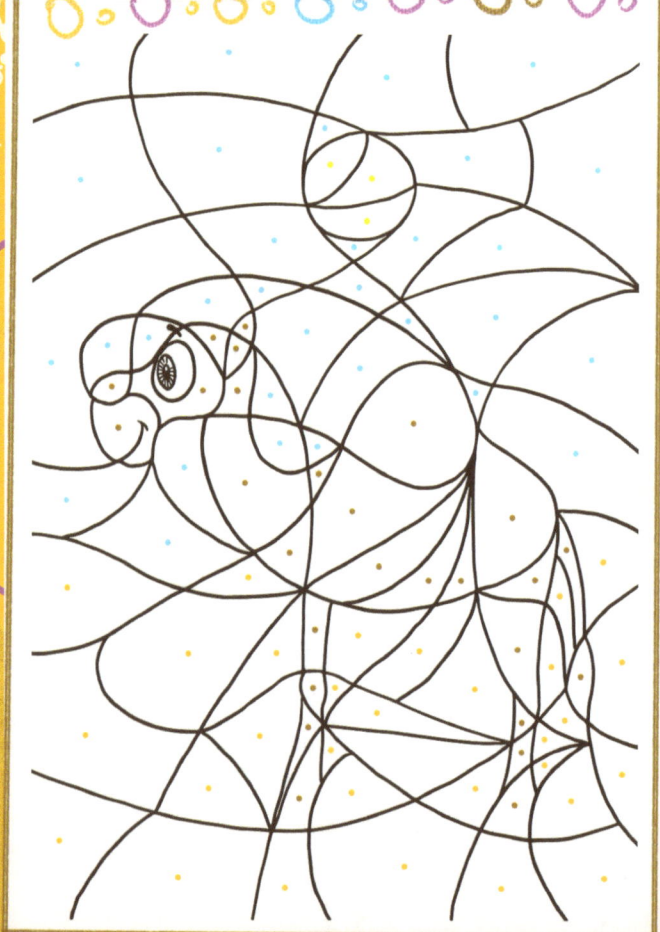

24

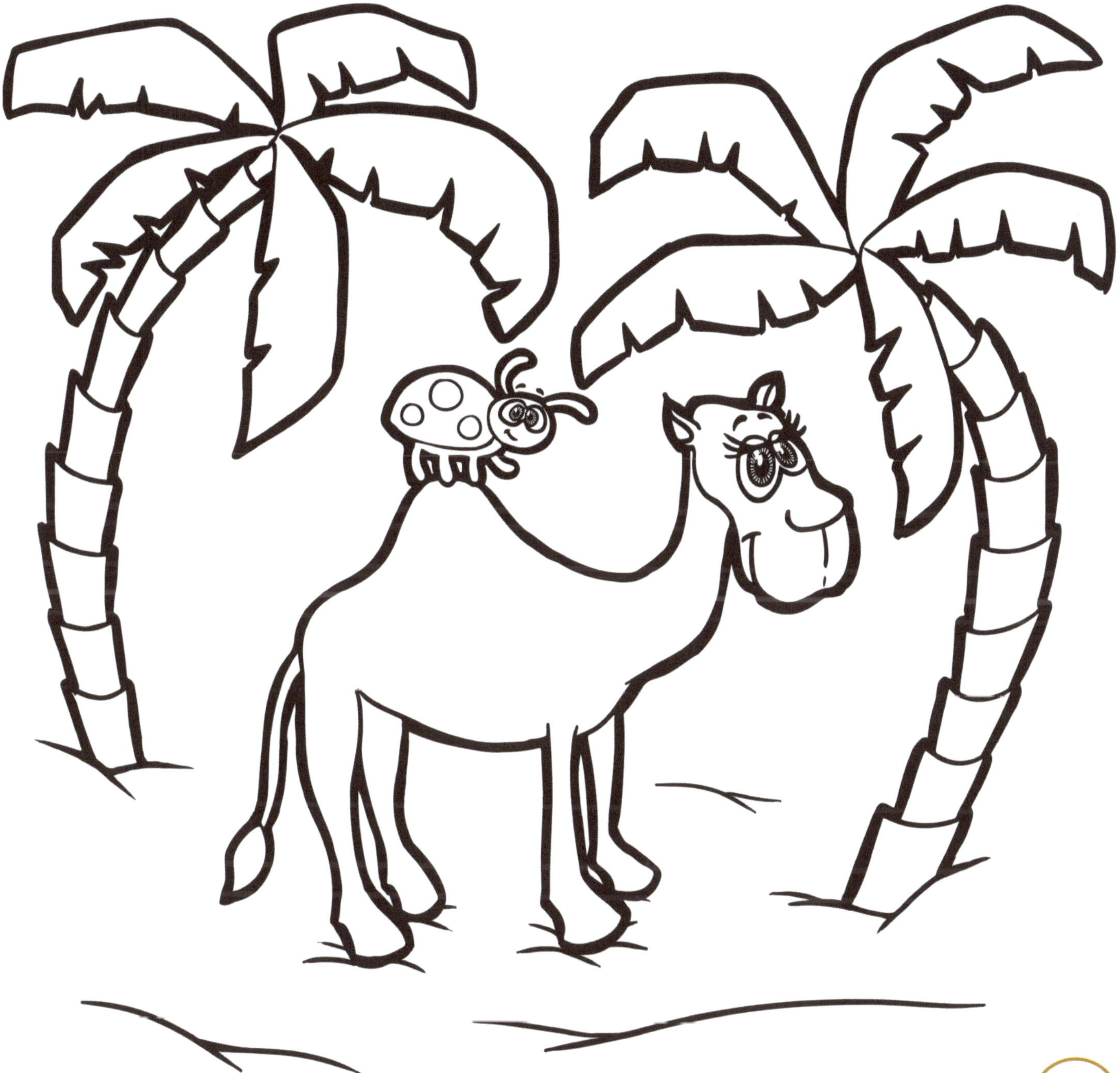

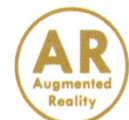

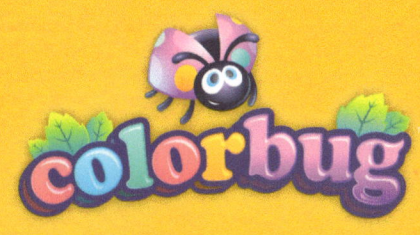

an augmented reality edutainment app that magically brings kids' storytelling and coloring books, to life!

getcolorbug.com

A space for your sketches, drawings and doodles

Meet Terrence

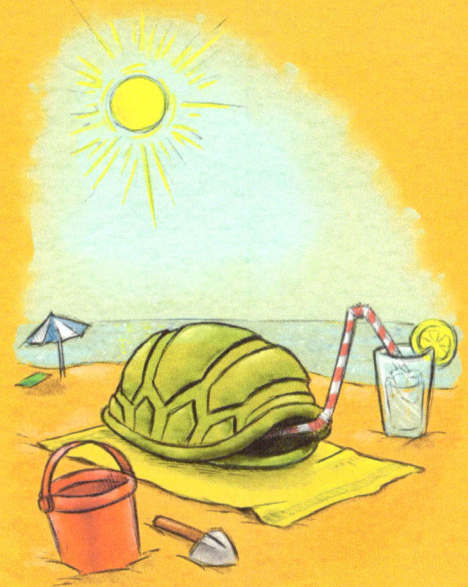

He likes the beach and the sun. He also spends a lot of time resting inside his shell, so he doesn't get sunburn. For this reason everyone thinks he's lazy and slow, but rumor has it that he even beat Ricky in a running contest once. Since it wasn't an official race there is no video evidence of it. Of course Ricky denies that he lost and Terrence never comments on this. He just puts on a mysterious grin when asked about it.

Hello, I'm Terrence!

Turtles

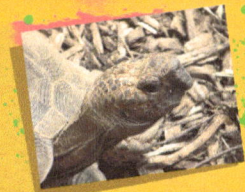 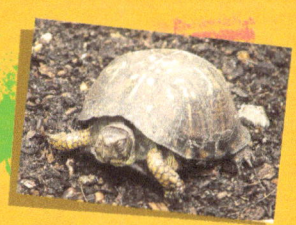

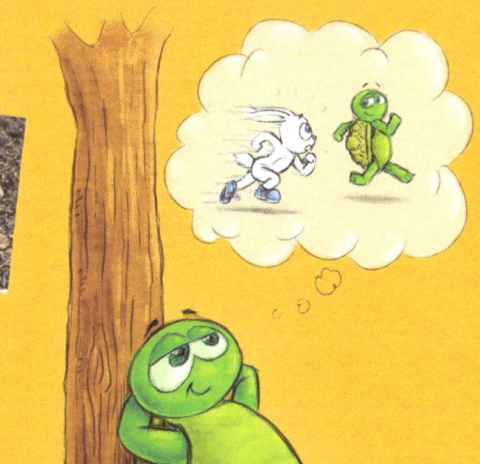

Turtles are reptiles characterised by a special bony or cartilaginous shell developed from their ribs and acting as a shield. The turtle's shell also has nerve endings in it. If you touch the shell, a turtle can feel it. The earliest turtles had teeth and they could not pull their heads into their shells.

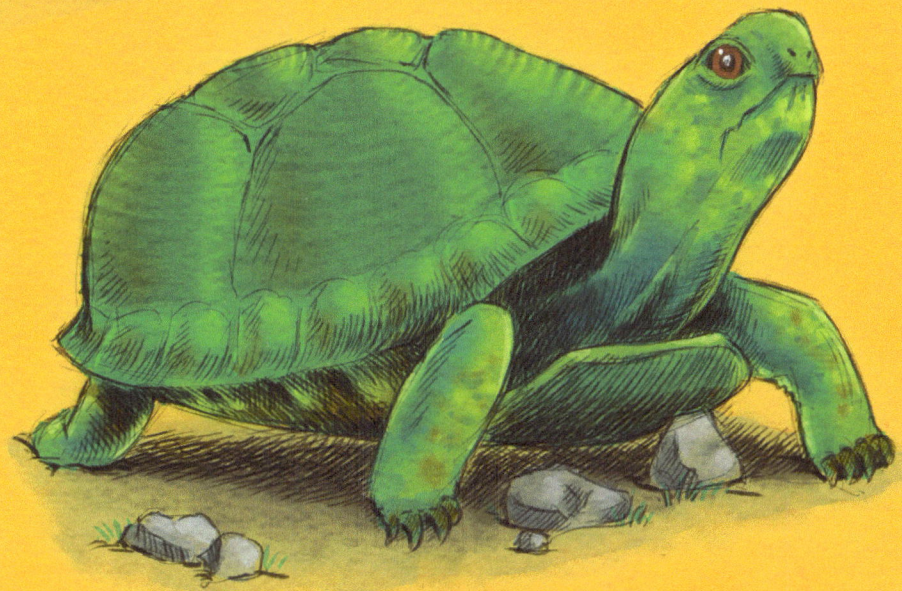

They have existed for around 215 million years. The largest turtle is the leatherback sea turtle, it can weigh over 900 kg! Turtles breathe air and do not lay eggs underwater, although many species live in or around water. They have rigid beaks, and use their jaws to cut and chew food.

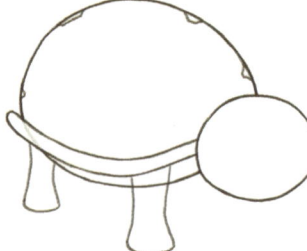

Draw your own Terrence following these steps!

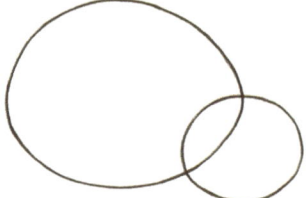
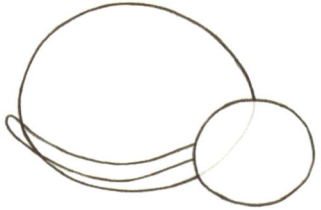

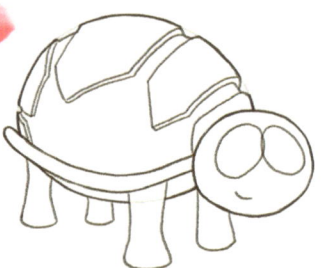
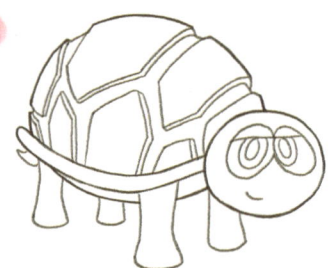
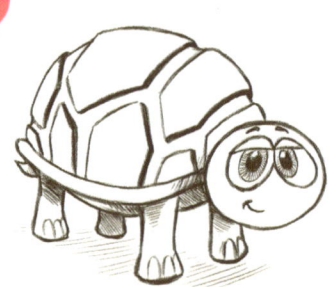

Write the exact time in the empty fields below each clock.

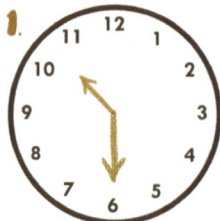
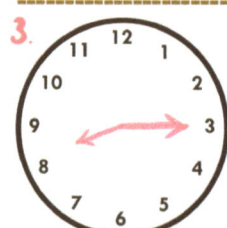
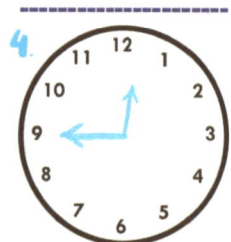
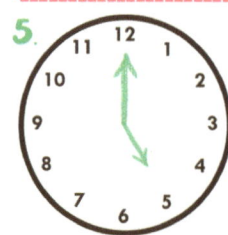
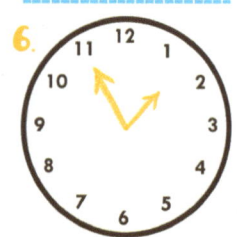

Circle the objects that you could find on a beach!

SURFBOARD HAT

SAND TOASTER SOFA

GLASS

TOOTHPASTE

TOWEL

SEAGULLS

SUNGLASSES SNOWMAN

POTATOES STARFISH

KEYBOARD COWS

SCISSORS

LAMP SHELLS

FLIPPERS STAPLER

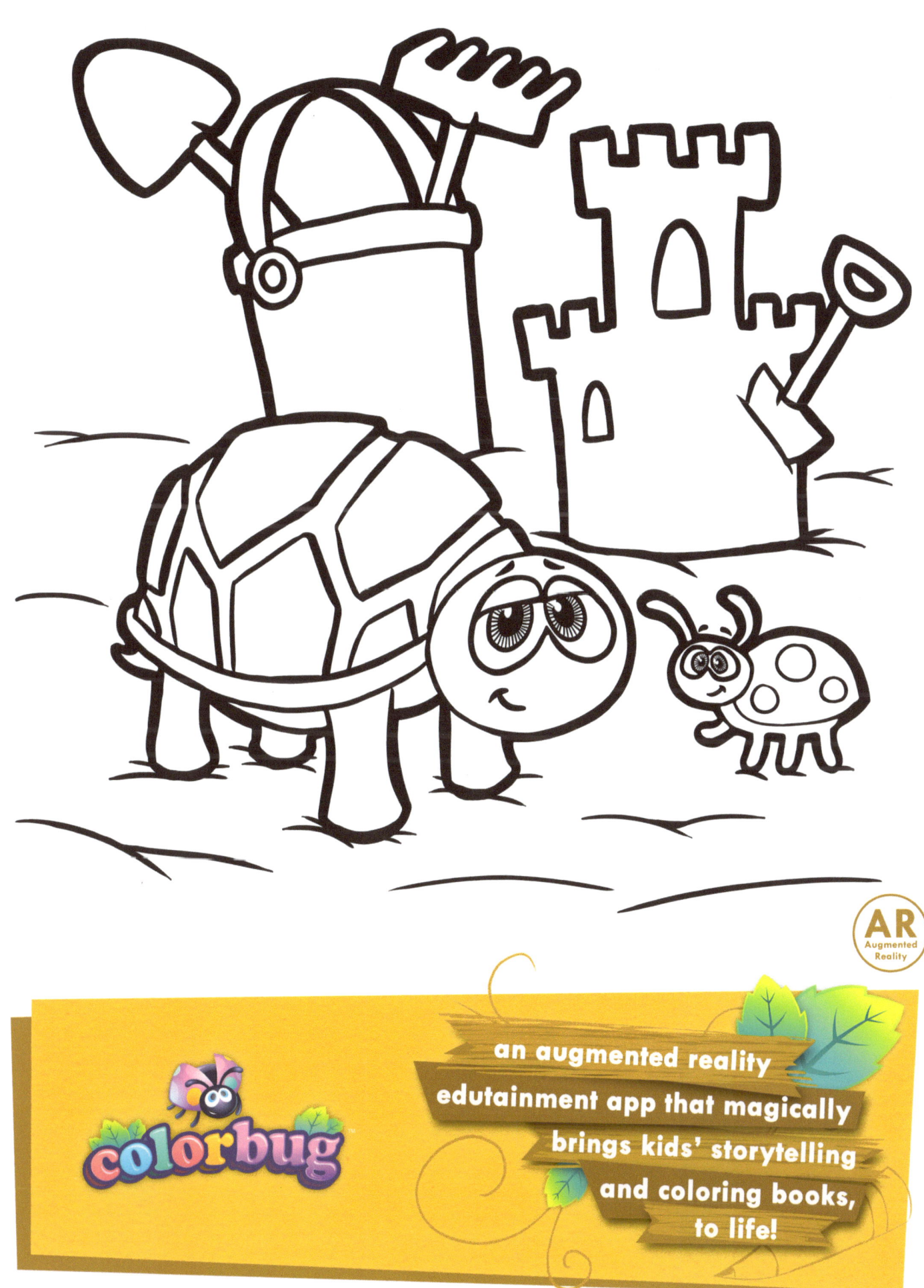

an augmented reality edutainment app that magically brings kids' storytelling and coloring books, to life!

colorbug

getcolorbug.com

AR
Augmented
Reality

A space for your sketches, drawings and doodles

Meet Fatah

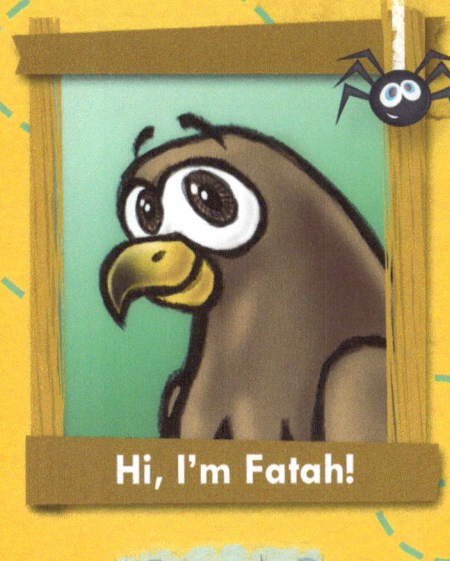

He lives in Dubai and is very popular there, like some kind of superstar. He loves to fly over the Dubai skyline and to admire its architecture and height. Every once in a while he tries to compete with the speed of Burj Khalifa's elevators, and sometimes he wins. He loves to do stunts in the air for his fans around Downtown Dubai. He also frequently visits Mushrif at his park. It only takes him 10 minutes to fly from Dubai to visit him in Abu Dhabi.

Falcons

Hi, I'm Fatah!

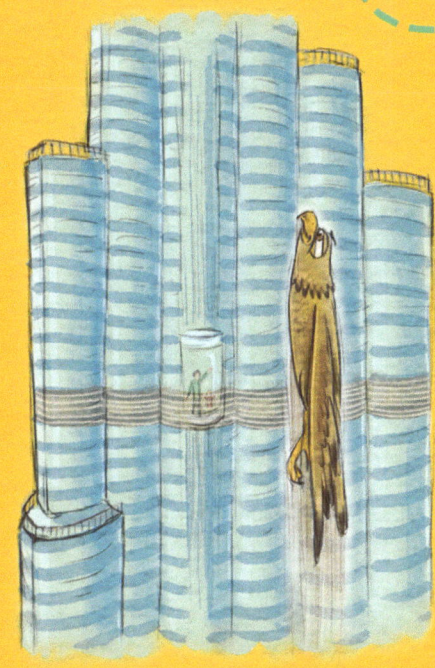

Falcons are raptors who hunt and eat animals for food. They are best known for their ruthlessness and their incredible flying abilities. There are more than 40 different species of falcons that can be found all around the world such as the peregrine falcon and the black falcon. The peregrine falcon is the most common bird of prey in the world and is found on every continent besides Antarctica. They can live up to 17 years.

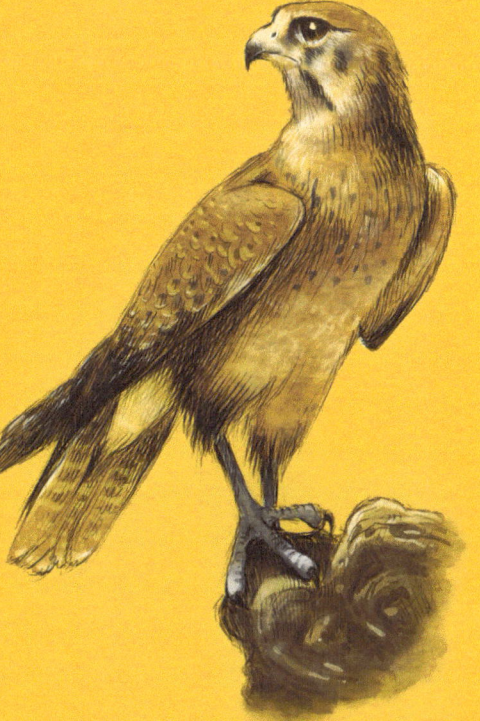

Falcons vary in size from 25cm tall to more than 60cm tall, but the height of the falcon depends on the species. The biggest ones live in Alaska. Peregrine falcons have been recorded diving at speeds of 200 miles per hour (320 km/h), making them the fastest-moving creatures on Earth.

Fun with Fatah

Draw your own Fatah following these steps!

 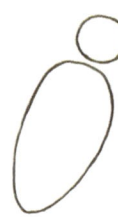 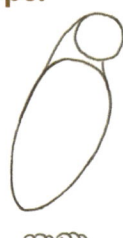 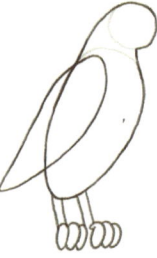 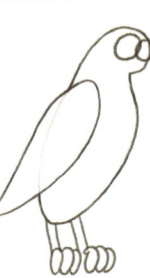 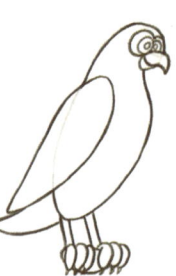 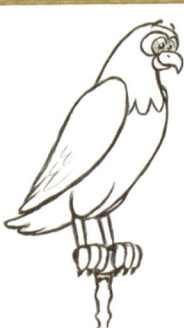

Can you read the words below?

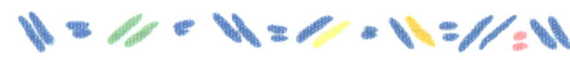

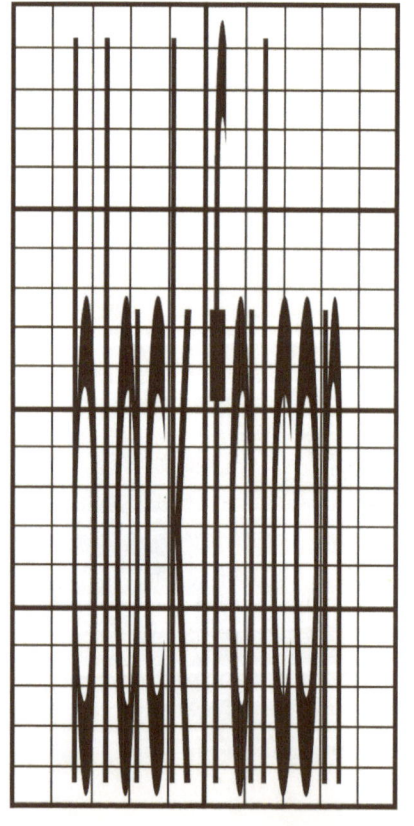

Answer the following questions, the answers are in the book.

1. Where is the Eiffel Tower located?

- -

2. How many bones do horses have?

- -

3. Who are the fastest-moving creatures on Earth?

- -

4. What do camels store in their humps?

- -

5. What kind of penguin is the tallest of all?

- -

6. How many spiders are there in this book?

- -

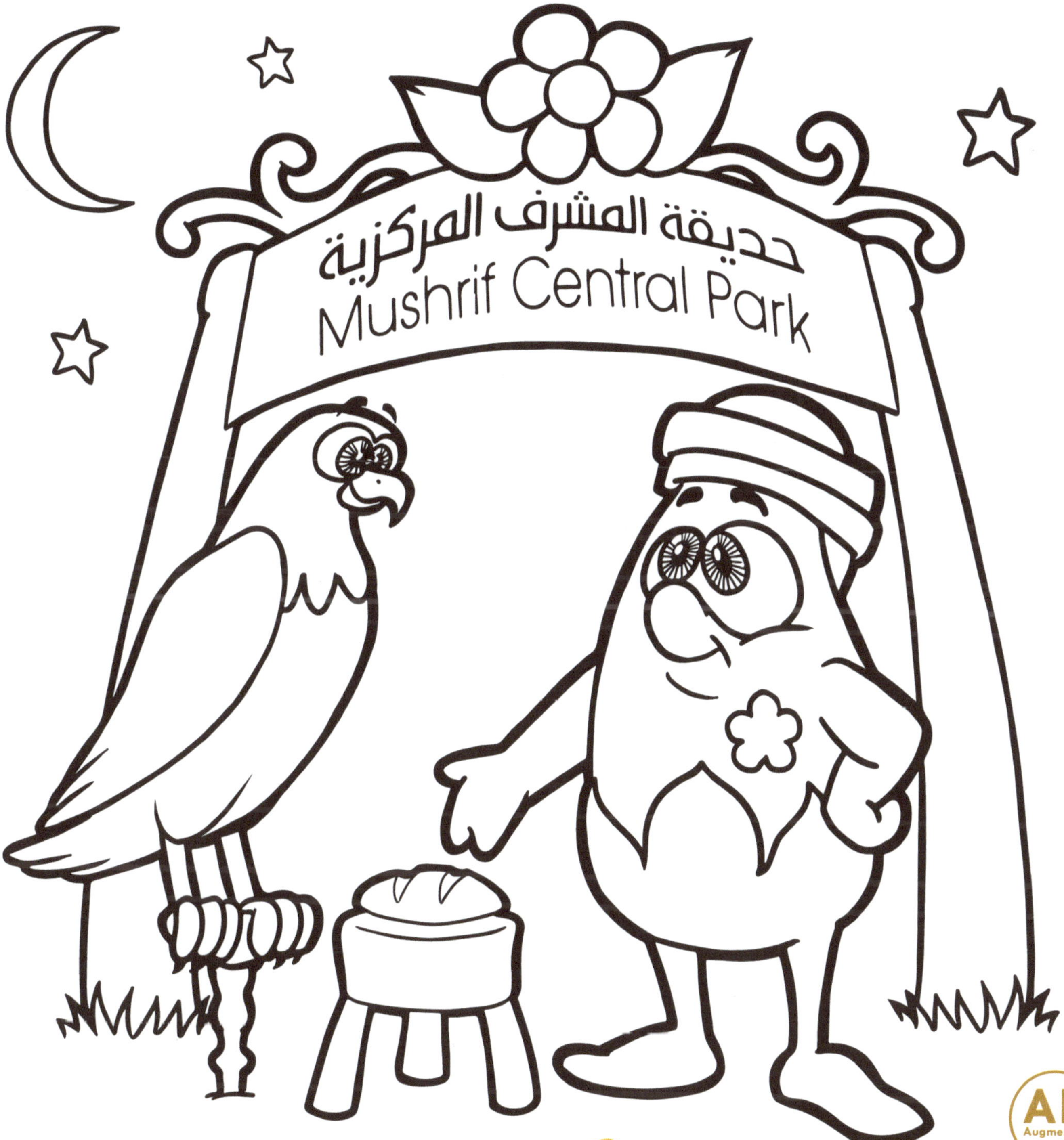

حديقة المشرف المركزية
Mushrif Central Park

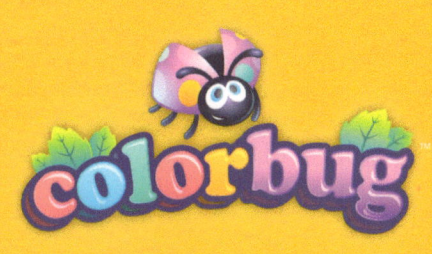

an augmented reality
edutainment app that magically
brings kids' storytelling
and coloring books,
to life!

AR
Augmented
Reality

getcolorbug.com

A space for your sketches, drawings and doodles

Fun With Bugsy - Spot 5 differences!

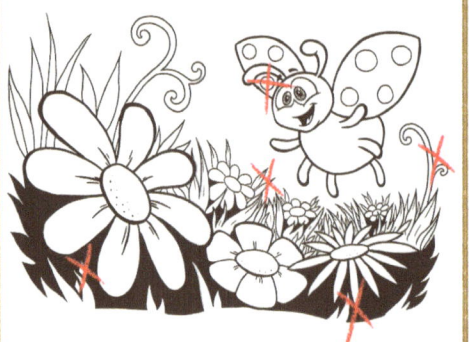

Fun with Ricky - Connect the pictures with the correct names!
1. Burj Khalifa 2. Pyramids of Giza
3. Statue of Liberty 4. Sydney Opera
5. Eiffel Tower

Fun with Mushrif - Every row, column and grid must contain all four of these images:

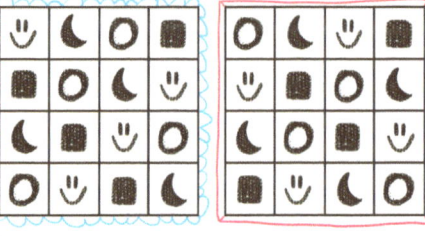

Decode the message:
A best friend is like a four leaf clover, hard to find, lucky to have.

Fun with Patrick - Help Patrick find his ball!

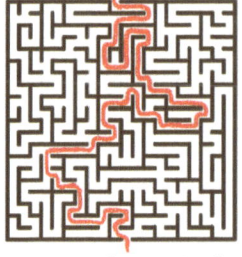

Take some watercolors, mix them and paint the circles with the colors that you get!
Colors in circles from top to bottom:
green, purple, orange, turquoise, brown

Fun with Pablo - Which two fish are the same?
Numbers 3. and 10.
Write down the names of the instruments!
From top to bottom: accordion, guitar, trumpet, saxophone, harp

Fun with Clemence - Find the words!

Color in fields using the colors of the dots.

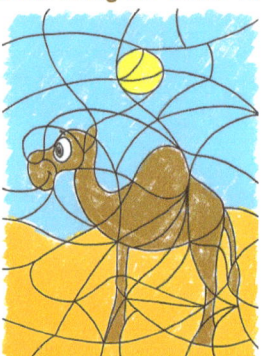

Fun with Terrence - Write the exact time in the empty fields below each clock.
1) 10:30 2) 2:25 3) 8:15
4) 12:45 5) 5:00 6) 1:55
Circle the objects that you could find on a beach!
sand, towel, sunglasses, flippers, shells, surfboard, hat, seagulls, starfish

Fun with Fatah - Can you read the words below?
black falcon
Answer the following questions, the answers are in the book.
1. Paris 2. Around 250 3. Peregrine falcons
4. Fatty tissue 5. The emperor penguin
6. There are 9 spiders in the book

Answers

Acknowledgements
This coloring book aims to expand kids' imaginations and bring smiles to faces all over the world!

Thanks to all those who believed in us from day one and helped turn this vision into reality, especially those who contributed in making colorbug an international app.

Special thanks to Maxine Denis who gave her voice to Bugsy and thanks to Ihsan El Eid, Brosso Ying, Pamela Kesrouani, Julianna Lai for helping to localize the app in different languages. Also the MIT Enterprise Forum, Touch Lebanon and Oqal KSA for providing us with much needed grants to keep us going and innovating.

Additional sources:
wikipedia.org
freestockphotos.biz
creativemarket.com/DmitriyChirkov
elfadophotoscape.blogspot.com.br

www.ingramcontent.com/pod-product-compliance
ightning Source LLC
mbersburg PA
W050406180526
CB00005B/2165